MILITARY MACHINES

FIGHTER JETS

By Michael Portman

Gareth Stevens
Publishing

Please visit our website, www.garethstevens.com. For a free color catalog of all our high-quality books, call toll free 1-800-542-2595 or fax 1-877-542-2596.

Library of Congress Cataloging-in-Publication Data

Portman, Michael, 1976-
 Fighter jets / Michael Portman.
     p. cm. — (Military machines)
 Includes index.
 ISBN 978-1-4339-8463-1 (pbk.)
 ISBN 978-1-4339-8464-8 (6-pack)
 ISBN 978-1-4339-8462-4 (library binding)
 1. Fighter planes—Juvenile literature. I. Title.
 UG1242.F5P66 2013
 623.74'64—dc23

                              2012024375

First Edition

Published in 2013 by
Gareth Stevens Publishing
111 East 14th Street, Suite 349
New York, NY 10003

Copyright © 2013 Gareth Stevens Publishing

Designer: Michael J. Flynn
Editor: Kristen Rajczak

Photo credits: Courtesy of the US Air Force: cover, pp. 1 by Senior Airmen Gustavo Gonzalez, 5 by Tech. Sgt. Michael Holzworth, 10–11 by Master Sgt. Michael Ammons, 11 by Staff Sgt. Darnell T. Cannady, 13 by Airman 1st Class Benjamin Gonsier, 14–15 by Airman 1st Class Dillon Davis,16 by Joe Oliva, 17, 18–19 by Staff Sgt. James L. Harper Jr., 20–21 by Josh Plueger, 23 by Master Sgt. Kevin J. Gruenwald, p. 24 by 1st Lt. Joel Cooke, 27 by Staff Sgt. Austin M. May, 29 by TSGT Justin D. Pyle; p. 4 Fox Photos/Hulton Archive/Getty Images; pp. 6–7 Hulton Archive/Getty Images; pp. 8–9 Roger Viollet/Getty Images; courtesy of the US Navy: pp. 24–25 by Phan Phillip A. McDaniel, 28–29 by Andy Wolfe.

Printed in the United States of America

CPSIA compliance information: Batch #CW13GS: For further information contact Gareth Stevens, New York, New York at 1-800-542-2595.

CONTENTS

Words in the glossary appear in **bold** type the first time they are used in the text.

FIRST FLIGHT

The ability to fly has always been one of humanity's greatest wishes. For centuries, stories have been told of the wonders and dangers of human flight. Meanwhile, inventors struggled to create machines that would allow humans to soar through the air. On December 17, 1903, the Wright brothers made that dream real.

Within a few years, airplanes were flying in countries around the world. It wasn't long before military leaders realized that an airplane could be an important weapon. Let's look at how the first fighter planes led to today's amazing fighter jets!

The Wright brothers' plane was the beginning of the age of human flight.

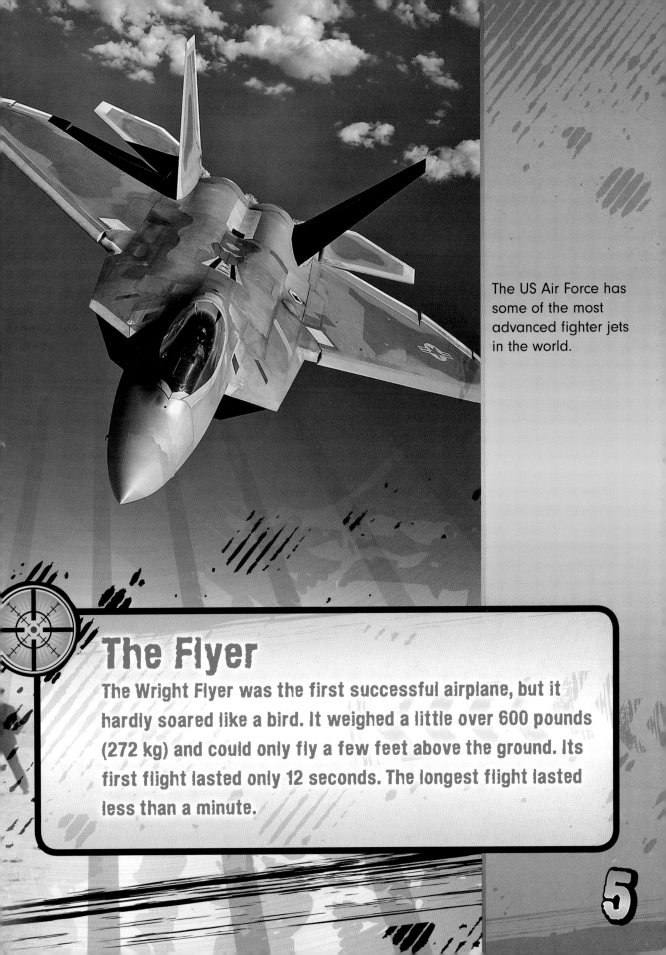

The US Air Force has some of the most advanced fighter jets in the world.

The Flyer

The Wright Flyer was the first successful airplane, but it hardly soared like a bird. It weighed a little over 600 pounds (272 kg) and could only fly a few feet above the ground. Its first flight lasted only 12 seconds. The longest flight lasted less than a minute.

FIRST FIGHTERS

Propellers powered the first fighter planes in World War I. Air battles, called dogfights, were fought at close range. Pilots fired machine guns that were mounted on planes made of **canvas** and wood.

Although the fighter planes of World War II were still powered by propellers, they were made of metal and could fly hundreds of miles per hour. Near the end of World War II, however, American and British pilots were surprised and afraid when a new type of plane attacked them. The new plane could fly extremely fast and didn't have propellers! It was the first fighter jet.

Speeding Ahead

At the start of World War I, fighter planes were relatively slow, flying at only 75 miles (120 km) per hour. Faster fighter planes had better chances in the deadly dogfights. As engine **technology** advanced, speed increased. In fact, by the end of World War I, the speed of fighter planes had increased by more than 50 percent.

At first, dogfights occurred between single planes. By the end of World War I, groups of planes called squadrons fought each other in special formations.

7

The first fighter jet was a German plane called the Messerschmitt Me 262. The Me 262 was **designed** in 1939 but didn't see **combat** until 1944. Armed with cannons and bombs, its top speed was about 540 miles (869 km) per hour. That made it faster than any other fighter! More than 1,400 Me 262 fighters were made, but only about 300 were used in combat. Fortunately for the Allies, the Me 262 was too late to help Germany win the war.

Even so, the Me 262 made all other fighter planes **obsolete**. After seeing it in action, America, Great Britain, and Russia began to work on their own fighter jets.

The Me 262 was one of the first planes to be powered by a jet engine.

Shooting Star

The Me 262 could fly about 120 miles (193 km) per hour faster than the best American fighter, the P–51 Mustang. The first US fighter jet was the P–80 Shooting Star. The Shooting Star never made it into combat in WWII but was used extensively in the Korean War.

WHAT IS A FIGHTER JET?

Fighter jets are one of the most important weapons in the military. They're small, fast, and **maneuverable**. They have to be ready for action at a moment's notice, day or night, and in all types of weather.

At first, fighter jets were designed mainly to attack enemy aircraft. Other planes were designed to attack targets on the ground and in the water. Today, the US has fighter jets that can do all this! Pilots of early fighter planes needed to see the enemy up close in order to attack. New technology, such as **radar** and "smart" weapons, has made most close-range fighting a thing of the past.

Fighter jets can be used to guide and protect larger, slower planes carrying supplies, bombs, or troops.

The Smart Sidewinder

The AIM-9 Sidewinder is a short-range, air-to-air **missile**. Sidewinder missiles have been used on fighter jets since the 1950s. A Sidewinder is a "smart" weapon able to detect and follow the heat from a jet engine. This allows a pilot to fire a Sidewinder and have plenty of time to fly away before it explodes.

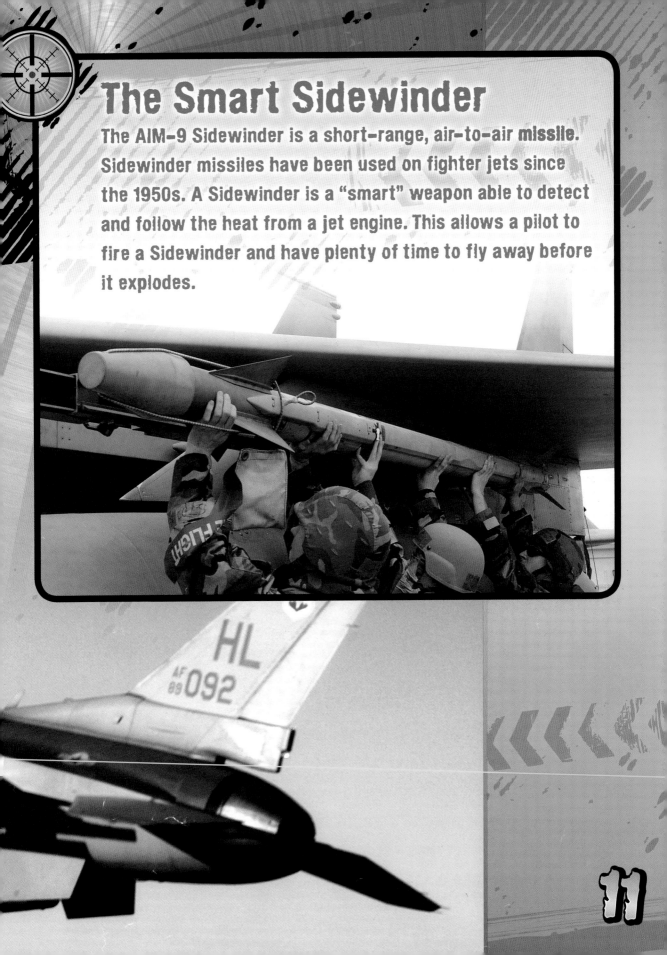

JET ENGINES

Fighter jets get their name because they're are powered by jet engines. Jet engines work by sucking in air through the front of the engine and forcing it out the back at a much greater speed.

A large fan draws air into the engine. Some of the air gets pushed together, or compressed. The compressed air is mixed with jet fuel, and a spark lights it in the engine's combustor. The burning gases spin a set of blades called a turbine, which keeps the front fan spinning. Finally, the burning gases shoot out the back of the engine, creating a force called thrust. Thrust pushes the airplane forward.

Engine Powered

Many people started experimenting with steam-powered aircraft during the late 1800s. However, the first successful airplanes were powered by the same kind of gas engines that power most cars. In 1930, a British pilot started working on the first jet engine. Its first successful flight didn't take place until 1937.

Jet engines are huge! Airmen train to work with them safely.

Not all the air that gets sucked into a jet engine is compressed. Some air flows around the moving parts of the engine. This helps cool the engine as well as reduce noise. The cooler air also adds thrust to the engine when it's mixed with **exhaust**.

Some jet engines have an afterburner. An afterburner adds fuel to the burning gases as they exit the engine. This creates even more thrust to help the fighter jet fly faster. The afterburner can only be used for short periods of time because it uses fuel very quickly.

Not Just for Jets

There are different types of jet engines. The engine described here is called a turbofan, which is the jet engine used by fighter jets. Helicopters use a jet engine called a turboshaft to spin their rotors. A ramjet is a type of jet engine that has no moving parts. Ramjets are mainly used in certain types of missiles.

Jet engines' afterburners, like this one, must be tested to make sure they'll work once the plane is in flight.

15

SOUND BARRIER

For many years, the speed of sound was seen as the greatest **barrier** in flight. Some people believed it was impossible to fly that fast. But that changed in 1947 when pilot Chuck Yeager became the first man to break the sound barrier.

"Mach" is the term that represents the speed of sound. When a plane flies fast enough to break the sound barrier, it's said to be traveling at Mach 1. As a plane's speed increases, so does its Mach number. For example, Mach 2 means twice the speed of sound. Planes that can fly faster than Mach 1 are called supersonic.

The speed of sound isn't always the same. It can change due to **altitude** and the temperature of the air.

Chuck Yeager's historic flight occurred on October 14, 1947.

Sonic Boom

When an airplane breaks the sound barrier, it creates a shock wave by pushing air aside with a lot of force. This creates a sound like a loud thunderclap called a sonic boom. A plane continues to make a sonic boom the entire time it flies at supersonic speeds.

17

G-FORCES

Today's fighter jets are the fastest planes in the world. Many are supersonic. Pilots who fly at these supersonic speeds deal with something called G-forces.

As fighter jet pilots dive through the sky, they might feel G-forces from different directions, including from head to toe or from front to back.

G-force is the measurement of the force of **gravity** or acceleration—the change of speed over time—on an object. When a person on the ground is standing still, they're experiencing one G-force. When an object rapidly speeds up, the G-forces, or "Gs," increase. Too many Gs can cause a person to faint.

Pilots wear special flight suits to help them deal with high G-forces. These suits allow them to handle up to nine Gs. That's nine times the force of gravity!

Feel the Thrill

If you've ever been pressed against your seat on a roller coaster, then you've felt the effect of G-forces. Roller coasters are designed to provide a safe amount of G-forces for a short amount of time. Ordinary things, such as sneezing and jumping, can create high G-forces. We just don't notice them because they don't last very long.

19

F-15 EAGLE

The F-15 Eagle is one of the best fighter jets ever made. Since its first flight test in 1972, the US Air Force has depended on this military machine. And for good reason—the F-15 has never been defeated in combat.

The F-15 Eagle was created only for air combat. The Strike Eagle model was designed to bomb targets on the ground as well as fight in the air.

The F-15 can reach Mach 2.5! Its wings, powerful engines, and fairly low weight make it very maneuverable. The F-15 may carry many different weapons, including machine guns and missiles. A "heads-up" display is one of the F-15 features that makes the jet excellent in combat. Important information is projected onto the windscreen so a pilot doesn't have to look down at the instrument panel!

Room for Two

The F-15 Strike Eagle is one model of the F-15 Eagle. Unlike the first F-15s, it has an additional seat for a weapons systems officer (WSO). The WSO is in charge of the F-15 Strike Eagle's weapons. Having a WSO allows pilots to give their full attention to flying.

F-16 FIGHTING FALCON

Since 1979, the F-16 Fighting Falcon has been used by both the air force and the navy. It can be flown night or day and in many conditions. The F-16 can fly long-distance missions of more than 1,000 miles (1,609 km) round trip.

The F-16, despite being small and lightweight, is very strong. It can withstand up to nine Gs! No other current fighter jet is capable of that. The F-16 also has advanced electronics to help with flight control. In the recent conflicts in Iraq and Afghanistan, the F-16 became an important part of the US military's air support.

F-16s Around the World

The F-16 is one of the most popular fighter jets. There have been almost 4,500 F-16s made for 26 different countries. In 2012, a new model of the F-16 was revealed to the public. The F-16V features many technological improvements designed to keep the Fighting Falcon flying for years to come.

The F-16 is known for its extraordinary combat radius, or the great distance that it's able to fly, fight, and then return to its base.

23

F/A-18 HORNET

The F/A-18 Hornet was made with a special purpose. It's both a fighter jet and an attack jet, which means it can take part in air combat as well as fly low to take out ground targets. The F/A-18 was the first US plane able to do both of these tasks.

The US Navy's Blue Angels Flight Demonstration Squadron flies F/A-18 Hornets in their exciting air shows.

Super Hornet

The Hornet adapts to whatever operation it's needed for. Most often, that means crews change the types of weapons it carries. The Hornet is highly maneuverable and strong enough to carry numerous bombs and missiles. In addition, the F/A-18 is fast. It can reach a top speed of Mach 1.7!

Super Powerful

The navy and marine corps have flown the F/A-18 since 1983. By 2002, an updated model of the F/A-18 called the Super Hornet was in service. The Super Hornet is bigger and more powerful than the regular Hornet. It's also able to travel greater distances and carry more weapons.

STEALTH

The F/A-22 Raptor is the US Air Force's newest stealth fighter. Stealth fighters have special features that allow them to locate and destroy targets without being detected. The F/A-22 Raptor's stealth technology is so advanced that it looks as small as a bumblebee on radar!

The F/A-22 is designed to attack both air and land targets. Its powerful engines are able to supercruise, or fly at supersonic speeds without using an afterburner. That means that it can fly fast without having to burn through a lot of fuel. Despite its extraordinary design, the Raptor has yet to be used in combat.

The Nighthawk

The F-117A Nighthawk Stealth Fighter was the world's first stealth aircraft. The surface of an F-117A is angled, which, along with other features, helped make it almost impossible to detect on radar. The F-117A became famous for its air excellence during the First Gulf War. It was retired from service in 2008.

Special paint on stealth fighters, such as the F-22 pictured here, helps keep radar waves from bouncing back to their origin.

27

FUTURE FIGHTER

The F-35 Lightning II, or Joint Strike Fighter, is the future of fighter jets. It will eventually replace the F-16, F/A-18, and AV-8B Harrier II. The navy, air force, and marine corps will all use the F-35.

The F-35 is designed to be dependable, easy to maintain, and adaptable to different operations. Because it will be replacing several different aircrafts, three models of the F-35 were built. One model is a fighter jet that takes off from a normal runaway. Another model can land vertically, like a helicopter. The third F-35 is smaller so it can be used on aircraft carriers.

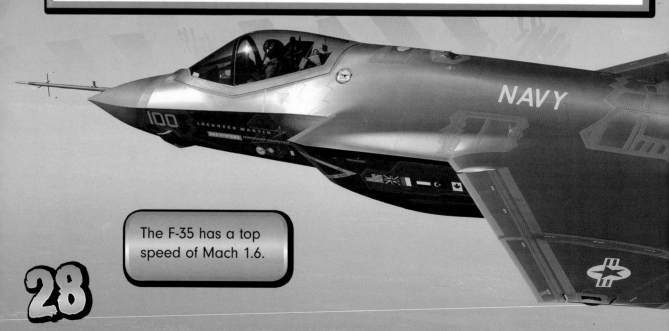

The F-35 has a top speed of Mach 1.6.

AV-8B Harrier II

Going Up!

The AV-8B Harrier II was the first jet to be able to take off and land vertically. That means the Harrier can operate in areas without a runway! The marine corps is the only branch of the US military to use the Harrier.

GLOSSARY

altitude: height above sea level

barrier: something that makes progress hard

canvas: a strong cloth

combat: armed fighting between opposing forces

design: to create the pattern or shape of something. Also, the pattern or shape of something.

exhaust: the gases that escape from the fuel burned in an engine

gravity: the force that pulls objects toward Earth's center

maneuverable: having the ability to be moved or steered very easily

missile: a rocket used to strike something at a distance

obsolete: outdated and no longer in use

propeller: paddle-like parts on a plane that spin to move the plane forward

radar: a way of using radio waves to locate and identify objects

technology: the practical application of specialized knowledge

FOR MORE INFORMATION

Books

Von Finn, Denny. *Jet Fighters*. Minneapolis, MN: Bellwether Media, 2010.

Zuehlke, Jeffrey. *Fighter Planes*. Minneapolis, MN: Lerner Publications Company, 2006.

Websites

Dynamics of Flight
www.ueet.nasa.gov/StudentSite/dynamicsofflight.html
Learn how airplanes fly and much more!

How Stuff Works: Modern Military Aircraft
science.howstuffworks.com/modern-military-planes-channel.htm?page=1
Learn all about many different types of military aircraft, including jets and helicopters.

Publisher's note to educators and parents: Our editors have carefully reviewed these websites to ensure that they are suitable for students. Many websites change frequently, however, and we cannot guarantee that a site's future contents will continue to meet our high standards of quality and educational value. Be advised that students should be closely supervised whenever they access the Internet.

INDEX